The Hard Part is Living.

"I did not die, and yet I lost life's breath."
-Dante Alighieri, The Divine Comedy.

Christabelle Marbun

To the ones who sat with me in silence,
This one's for you.

The Hard Part is Living

Christabelle Marbun

Oddities.

The light hits the grass so gently,
The summer breeze seemed to pass
through her.
Everything was existing,
And for the first time,
She's sad to leave.

She was of Dark Matter.

She existed, but that was all.
But she loved it,
every second of simply existing.
She danced between the lines,
Lived between the moments,
And walked amongst Dark Matter.
She seemed to have never wanted
Anything more,
she was content.

<u>Life Lessons from a Toothbrush.</u>
I had a blue toothbrush

when I was younger,

I would get so excited in

the morning to brush my teeth.

But after a couple of months,

 we had to get a new one. I hated the

thought of letting go of

my blue toothbrush,

Then it said to me,

"It's okay to say goodbye, things change

sometimes. And change isn't always bad,

sometimes it's healthy. Although we may

never meet again, I promise you'll grow"

So I parted with my blue toothbrush, losing

my first friend, but gaining a lifelong

lesson.

"How was your day?"

"I almost didn't have one."
"Good, and you?"

<u>The Books With the Lovely Covers.</u>

You see them on shelves, too eye-catching to miss. Those simple leather covers, soft to the touch, wonderful to hold.

Those are the ones with interesting stories, the ones with excellent grammar and captivating words.

They are the ones where you need not read between the lines.
The ones where you need not worry about understanding.

Those are the ones whose words seem to dance on the page,
The ones that remind you of your worth.

They are the fires you want to touch,
The pages you want to drown in.

Those are the ones where you can judge by their covers,
The ones with the lovely covers.

See them?
Those are the lives you want to know.

If I die,

Listen to my playlists.
Read my words.
And love like hell is your final
destination.

You will find me there.

How have i missed the sun for days in
a row?
i'm sorry, i never meant to lock
myself in here for far too long.
i wanted to get out of bed,
But i'm sick.
Of course you won't see it,
it's hidden behind the endless stacks
of water bottles in the corner,
The messy room, the clothes on the
chair, the unmade bed,
and the empty girl.
i'm sorry, everything is just really
bright right now.
So i'm seeking refuge in the dark.

If only time were a social construct,

Then some would have the choice not
to believe it.

Do you think the sun
has ever envied the moon?
So far away, the sun. So alone.
Bright, but alone.
The center of the universe, but alone.
Alone, but perhaps also lonely.
For the moon has us.
But the sun,
The sun shines,
Without ever asking for
anything in return.

I never really had nice handwriting,
But I tried to change.
Because maybe if I changed my
handwriting to be like her,

You'll love me like her too.

<u>Thirteen.</u>

I spent my thirteenth birthday
at the library.
I celebrated in the
crannies and nooks.
Surrounded by others
who were once thirteen too,
But made it to the History books.

No, ignorance is not bliss.
Saying that seems to justify the
action.
It's unfair.
Ignorance is numbness,
Ignorance is false,
Ignorance is *not* bliss.

Ignorance is Ignorance.

<u>City of Stars.</u>

I had forgotten what it felt like to overlook the city, The city that has something everybody wants. I fell in love with the warmth, the buildings, the lights, and everything abnormal about this city. If you look close enough, the alleyways have art, and every person has that light in their eyes, the ones you see when there's a promised dream.
No matter what happens here, the heartbreak or the victory,
I will always love it.
I stand outside of the observatory, while others were looking at the stars, I fell in love with the ground I walked on.
The city hugs me with passion and vibrance, like a soundtrack to a timeless movie.
This is the city that many run to.
This is it.
This is home.
The bustling of the crowd started to fade behind me, And I stood on that hill overwhelmed with beauty.
Because oh right,
It's lovely where I live.

What do you think
would have happened
if you never learned
to love the stars?

Don't worry,
Your mind is a beautiful thing.
Don't try to run away from it.
This is a letter from me to you.

(You will be just fine)

"I've missed you,
When will you be back?
You promised you would get better,
You promised you would come again.
So where have you been?
You used to love it here.
The tree stood perfectly above you,
shielding you from the rest of the
world.
When will you be back?
I've missed you."

-The bench across the swings

You lose things all the time.
Keys,
Wallets,
time,
And people.
I usually try retracing my steps,
Go back and see where things went wrong.
So I did.
I retraced the texts, the paragraphs, the endless
calls,
And the voicemails.
But I couldn't find you.
I missed a call from you, once.
I should have picked up,
Because maybe if I did,
I wouldn't have to retrace anything.
I miss you.
But you no longer walk amongst the searching.
I kept retracing,
     And retracing,
        And retracing.
Nothing.
But it's okay,
Because, well,
You lose things all the time

You have to learn to love a curse,
Until it becomes a blessing.

I would give it all to you if I could.
I would bottle up everything
for you to know what it means
to be alive.
All of it.
The happy, the hurt, and
infinite-in-between.
You will learn to pick your battles
And lose some of them,
Often to yourself.
Your fascination with
the world will
undoubtedly bring
about your downfall,
But you already knew that
And you live anyway.
So, of course, I would bottle it all up
I would,
For you.

Strength shouldn't be measured
by the number of times you can
fight someone or the invincibility
of something. But rather the amount
of times you get back up after life
has hurt you over and over, and
learn to love again.

She wasn't special,
For if she truly were,
You wouldn't be reading about a girl
who wants to change the world,
But is too scared she wouldn't
do it right.

Being Awake hurts you,
It hurts to breathe sometimes.
And yet I still go on car rides in
a desperate attempt to feel alive.
Because although being
Awake hurts you,
Oh,
 the things you would do to feel
infinite anyway.

<u>Here's to Foolish Endeavors.</u>

So I suppose this is it? All of the times
you have deemed yourself special
has led you here.
And what did you find? Nothing.
Absolutely nothing.
You believed you were different.
Your pursuit of becoming different
has led you to a dead-end *(literally)*.
You tried to fight, but it didn't
work did it now?
But I must give you this,
You know how to feel.
You know how to feel
very well, actually.
So you may not be special,
but you make everyone
else believe they are.
And that sets you apart.

Destined to be a Dickinson

She wrote,
She wrote with everything she knew
and loved with everything she was.
She wrote because that's all she knows,
Because she was hurting, and she knew words
could hurt.
She wrote because that was the only way
the world could make sense.
Writing promised her a better life,
instead, she found endless blank pages for her
to find herself.
She wrote until her blood became ink,
until her pain was displayed for all to see.
The world saw it and fell in love
with her flaws.
Slowly, she became nothing but metaphors.
Her writing less magical, life had left her eyes.
But she still put everything she had left onto
paper, all the love and loss, in hopes that others
would get to lead the life she was promised.
She wrote,
She wrote until they loved her.
It's a shame, though.
How she never realized,
that she was destined to be a Dickinson

I hope one day you will look in the
mirror again.
I hope you will look at yourself and
fix your hair but think
nothing much about it.
I hope you don't examine your flaws
and pick apart
the pieces you wish had broken off.
I hope you will learn to look at
yourself as if you are the entire world.
I hope one day you will look in the
mirror again.

I have learned much ever since
I started watching the grown-ups.
I have learned that they often want
control, but not the responsibility
that comes with it.

The misunderstood oddities
of the world had a place in her book.

So tell me,
how does one
un-align
the stars?

Exhaustion.

She always forgot to
clean her glasses,
So it was a bit blurry to her.
The line between
healthy and surviving.

I have come to believe,
That it is our belief in
a heavenly afterlife
that makes our lives
living hell.

They're the different ones, you see.
It's in their eyes.
They carry worlds on their shoulders.
Be kind,
For without them, we would have
no world to love.

True monsters are the ones who are
not afraid of the light.

Don't cry,
It will get better.
Home will get better.

I started reliving the same days,
But that wasn't the problem.
The problem was that the days
were never actually the same.

I just stopped noticing.

The art of being alive is
unmatched in its beauty.
Being alive is the best example
Of how beauty is in the eye of
The beholder.

A light is just as bright
as its darkness.

Living in a dark world is hard,
But living in a world without light is
harder.

I wanted so desperately to feel this
"alive" that everyone has
been talking about.
So I wonder,
When was the last time I lived
not for the sake of being alive?

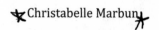

There was never truly a
good reason to stay,
just a million reasons not
to go through with it.

I missed the days when
miracles were common.
Days when a wonderful
happening was right
around the corner.
But alas, I have learned
that something is extraordinary
because it does not stay forever.
So on the days when
miracles are common,
I must prepare for the ordinary
to happen next.

She knew the pain all too well,
It was written between the lines
of her story.

My darling, that's the problem.
You tried so hard to
find a reason to live,
you died trying.

I would like to meet
more of myself one day.
I would like to see myself
for the very first time
and learn to love what you would.

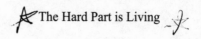

Progress is not noticing
when the song you used to cry to
is playing in the background.

Nobody has hurt her,
Nobody has left her.
For Nobody was a myth,
and she was not as clever as
Odysseus.

I hope you realize someday,
that your life is just as valuable
as the person you wish to be.

"Take your time"
They said.

She hung up the phone and sighed,
Knowing that time has given up on
her, a long time ago.

So don't tell her to breathe as if
it were an easy task.
Because there was a time when the
pain suffocated her.

She was in love with everything that exhausted her.

After years of fighting, I realized.
I had to stop fighting like I had
nothing to lose,
I had to start fighting like I had
something to fight for.

For I Will Not Slow Down for Life.

I'm not one to be marveled by the wonderful
things.
I appreciate them, of course, but I am fascinated by
the worst.
The good is simple, it warms your heart then you
move on.
But the bad is complicated, it hurts but it stays and
demands you to learn.
I have come to know that so much of the darkness
is untouched.
And so I promised myself, I will walk into the good
and bad
with an open heart; steadfast in my journey.

For I will not slow down for life,
So it kindly sped up for me.

I keep running and running until I have exhausted
my heart.
I apologized to pain because it is so hated.
I apologized for making its job of teaching me very
hard.
And with life by my side,
I will run into the field of hurt without an ounce of
selfishness.
I will learn and grow, I will grow but not change.
Then, maybe then,
I will learn to truly love the lavender and dark skies
all the same.

She wanted to be fixed,
but she didn't cry for help.
She never said why.
But the truth is,
You only cry for help
when you believe there is
help to cry for.

So hold her,
Just hold her.
Even when she refuses you,
Hold her.
Hold her until she falls apart.
She needs it.
She needs to break in order to
put herself back together again.

Was she poetry?
She thought.
Or was she merely
Glorified words?

She thought she had
felt true exhaustion.
But she was wrong.
It was this,
It was when being
exhausted felt like
a tiresome activity.

Even the bathroom floor was tired
of seeing her like this.

You are exhausted, I know.
But when will you realize that the
pain is valuable?
Just remember,
Your tears will grow flowers
And your heart will start fires.

At this point,
Authentic happiness
seems far more artificial
than faking it.

Death.

How selfish Life can be,
It will zip you around the universe
Then push you into the sun.
It will take you to lovely places
Then blind you for fun.
It will grab you by the heart and show
you how to fly,
Then throw you off a cliff, leaving you
to die.
And when it is done with you,
it will throw you on Death's door,
Broken, torn, and shaken to your core.
But Death will take you in
And hold you by the fire.
For it knows deep down,
That life is a liar.
It will hold you so tight,
Even if you refuse.
It will not harm you one bit,
For it knows you have
nothing left to lose.

I hope you live,
But not so much that
you're terrified of death.

Exhausted of Life's yelling,
I answered the door.
And there stood Death,
waiting for me.
Death stood there in the moonlight,

And she was beautiful.

When all the poems
have been written
And all the metaphors said,
What do you think
will become of her?

Mon, Jun 29,2020

"Don't die on me, okay?
That's all I'm asking.
Please promise me."

"I won't, I'm better now"

Tue, Jun 30, 2020

"You promised."

She's trying, she really is.
It's just getting harder and harder,
To write with poison ink and put her
life on paper.
She is trying to fix herself, drawing
little hearts and stars,
Strategically placing them on her
arm, over the cuts and scars.
So please understand that it is hard to
go farther,
It is hard for her to live, in a world
that has lost its wonder.

I was alone.
Completely and utterly alone.
I was silent and lonely,
With no one around to see.
So don't tell me I was wrong
to take the hands of death,
For I was alone,
And Death showed me kindness.

 Christabelle Marbun

Mother always said that I was made
of stardust,
She said it like a compliment.
Stardust, so beautiful yet so forgotten.
Mother glorified stardust,
She thought it was something special.
But Mother never realized,
Stardusts are merely the leftovers of
something that was once beautiful.

I suppose we all have our flaws,
Our own twisted story of the happy
sunshiney things.
I look up to the sky and see a
marvelous sight,
And to my surprise,
The clouds told a fairytale
And the stars painted a tragedy.

I hope you remember that
you can battle anything,
Whether it's the world
Or your own universe.

11/13/19

I remembered it well.
The way my hands were shaky,
The music of dead silence,
Even my breath seemed quiet.
My heart knew this feeling all too well,
It had already accepted my fate.
I remembered it well.
My bottled up emotions had formed
themselves into a bottle of pills.
The sound of my tears hitting the floor
served as a symphony to my death.
I knew that I wasn't a hero, I was hardly
ever a good friend to myself.
I remembered it well.
I closed my eyes in a desperate attempt to
be anywhere but the bathroom.
But my mind didn't want to be
anywhere else,
This was home.
I had been through hell long enough to
get comfortable.
I remembered it well.
I uncapped the bottle and emptied it out,
Mindlessly counting every single pill
on my hand,

Then capped the bottle and twisted it,
Sealing my fate.
I knew what was coming,
I knew the outcome.
I remembered it well.
The stack of letters in the corner
was urging me now.
I was ready.
I was ready to leave behind
the broken shards of myself
That people desperately tried
to put back together.
I was ready.
I remembered it well.
The last fleeting cry of hope I let out.
But nothing came.
I hope you know I fought,
with everything I had.
I hope you also know that
sometimes we lose.
And I hope,
That you remember me well.

You keep reminding me of the
wonderful things to try
and get me to stay.
I know that they're wonderful,
I know how lovely
the sunsets can be.
I'm not asking you to remind me of
all the things I would miss
because I know I'll miss them.
I have fought for those things, I
fought for another day.
I kept trying because
I wanted to see the ocean
and watch the stars with you.
But at the end of the day, I am asking
you one simple favor,
Please stop reminding me of them,
Please don't make me
want this again.

What do you think it means to live?
I think it means feeling
everything, even the nothing.
It means knowing the quiet
and understanding the chaotic.
I think it means waking up again
after crying yourself to sleep.
I think it means being
human, in all its faults.
Being messy, getting hurt,
fall in love, and everything
else in between.
I think it means feeling infinite
and mortal simultaneously.
I think it means being
in love with the tiring things.
It means accidentally staying up late.
And perhaps accepting our reality,
whether flawed or broken.
I think it means dancing
between the lines.
I think, in its truth,
it means all the colors at once,
In full brightness.

It wasn't that she
didn't want to live,
It was that she had
fallen for death.

I had packed away my youth in a
small red box.
I watched it die that day.
I put it in a small red box and said my
goodbyes,
Then tucked it under my bed
Never to be seen again.

She stood across her and asked,

>"Why do you take so long to
>come for me?"

Death smiled,
>"You're quite impatient. Others
>spend their lives
>trying to outrun me."

She looked at death
longingly and said,
>"I've met life,
>I wasn't impressed."

She tries,
You can see that on her arm,
Through the hearts she had
strategically drawn over the scars

You taught me how to love deeply,
You taught me how to wonder,
You taught me that
the world was bright.
You always said that
it will all be okay,
That if it's ours to have,
it will fall into place.
You told me who I was,
and you taught me to love it.
Until one day,
There was nothing.
Everything was silent.
And although I was miles away,
I knew.
I didn't know who I was looking at
in the mirror,
That's when I knew you were gone.
And I realized that after all this time,
You were teaching me how to let go.

She was a powerful force,
She moved the skies and tamed the
oceans.
One day, there was nothing.
Just then the world stood still.
The oceans fell silent,
And the heavens went dark.
The galaxies raged
The stars mourned.
For the universe had just lost
One of their brightest lights.

I listen to the tapes everyday now.
I hear her laughter, I can almost hear
her smile.
This time it hurt, hearing her again.

She was there,
Then she wasn't.

I miss it.
The days when the grass was greener
And the paintings were brighter.
I listen to the tapes everyday now.

When you were there,
Before you weren't.

The art of loving the
world was dying.
It was dying along with her.
I stopped noticing the
silly drawings on the wall,
I rarely laughed at people
tumbling in the ice rink.
I hadn't realized that the
sun sets much earlier now,
I forgot to make sandcastles
at the beach.
Then I realized that I had
lost you a long time ago,
But just like the wonderful
things of the world,
I stopped noticing.

I never payed attention on survival,
I started searching for why to instead.

You were one to go on adventures,
You'd wander off in the dark.
I would run after you there,
following you with a spark.
One that I lit with my bare hands,
And kept aflame with my heart.
But this time I had lost you,
I had lost you to the dark.

Death didn't invite me in,
It hardly ever saw me.
It was never death that brought me
along,
It was life that drove me away.

So no matter the heartbreak,
no matter the victory,
I hope you know that
Death is not the end,
And your tale
will not be a tragedy.

A Love Letter to Death.

You are wonderful, in all your grandeur, you
are wonderful.
Life gets all the praise, but for now, it will step
aside in humility.

Hello, Death. It is wonderful to meet you.
Chin up, my darling, I know you are not loved
by many.
But for whatever this is worth, you are deeply
loved by one.

You never take, you simply accept,
You accept the ones life had hurt
And done its damage to.

You wait in patience, and dance with time.
As you watch life become romanticized,
Without an ounce of envy.

You know that in the end, those who have ran
with life,
Will have to walk with you,
To the end of time.

So chin up, my darling, you are kind.
For you are wonderful, in all your simplicity,
You are wonderful.

After existing on this slow-moving
hour glass for merely one second,
I have come to three conclusions:

1. Time is one of the most ruthless
   teachers, but you learn.
   Whether willingly or
   unwillingly, you learn.
2. Life can sometimes be the
   enemy, as bright as it claims to
   be.
3. Death can be dark, but it can be
   your dearest friend.

I have two clocks in my room,
They both tick rhythmically,
Counting down the seconds
Until the day you come for me.

You are no longer here,
I can't feel you with my touch.
But I am not worried,
In fact, I'm relieved.
For although you are no longer here,
I know,
You are with an old friend.

(Death)

Deep down she'd known,
This was the final time
her eyes would shut.
But where she's going,
she needs no eyes to see,
For you are guiding her,
Towards immortality.

Christabelle Marbun

Love.

I hope you notice the falling leaves as
they hit the ground today,
And I hope you learn to smile when
you hear the children play.

I hope you look up to the sky and see
the clouds up there,
How one is shaped like a bird, and the
other one a bear.

I hope one day you will pick up your
heart and put it on display,
And not fear pain or be to scared to
give it all away.

I hope that even when you work you
will hum or twirl your pen,
In the end, I truly hope, you will fall
in love with life again.

Of course you love her,
She's everything good about the
world.

I had found out the truth a
long time ago,
The moment life hit,
That I was one,
to write of love
But never truly know it.

Oh the pain of loving agony.
It's the cruelest form of love, truly.
The pursuit of feeling infinite is an endless task
that leaves its searchers empty.
I long for the day when the clouds shall return
to the sky and bring my tears
along with them as rain,
And I hope that I will be of sunsets.
Oh the pain of loving agony,
It ties me to the hurt with a rope
I weaved myself,
It's truly destructive, in its nature, but I have no
means to overpower it.
For I could sit all day on this roof and reach my
hands up to the skies,
But my breath will always tie me down and
gravity will lock unto my heartbeat,
never letting go.
Oh the pain of loving agony.
It begins the cycle of loving the love I
disapprove of loving,
It shows me that in the end, when the finish
line welcomes me with open arms, that I will
be released from this very cell I kin.
The sun will set in my eyes and
the heavens will rise in me.
I will no longer breathe poison.
Oh the pain of loving agony.

You were everything
perfection could not touch.

Her emotions were powerful,
She rationalized the unjust.
She went to great lengths to prove
Nothing to no one.
A person's mind could be relatively
powerful,
But one's emotions could do things
the mind
Could only dream of.

<u>In Fear of Falling in Love.</u>
I made sure I didn't ruin anything. I
taught myself to say the right things.
I made sure that we were never alone,
I made sure I didn't laugh too hard at
your jokes. I did it all.
I made sure that I wouldn't look at
you for too long in fear of
falling in love.
I didn't tell you because I knew that
you'd do anything for me.
You would do anything to make me
happy, because you cared.
If I told you I loved you, you would
try so hard to love me too.
But you won't, because you can't.
Then you'd lie to yourself and say
that you love me too. For you are too
stubborn to admit that love cannot be
summoned, and you will keep trying
because that is your way,

I ran so far away from you that I
couldn't seen your flaws;
you were perfect.
Although you were not, I liked to
think you were.
So I will love you from afar,
and that will have to do.
Because if Eponine had
taught me anything,
it is that love demands sacrifice
and pain demands to be felt.

I looked at you, no, into you.
I saw through your eyes and
into your mind.
I knew that heartbreak was next,
but you were still talking.
And when you speak,
the universe seemed to lean in,
As if it had never seen
anything like you.
I wanted you to know that,
before you broke my heart.
I wanted you to know that
the universe has never
seen anything like you.

I hope that one day
You will be bright with someone.

I became so used to it,
I welcomed pain like a friend,
And turned love away at the door.

It's one of the most painful things,
To watch two people who once
vowed to spend the rest of their lives
together,
become complete strangers.

Unless it is My Own.

I sat in the darkness of time,
In my own world-
paperbacks of words I won't say.
When I learned to fall for myself,
I kissed the sky- and I was infinite.
In another lovelier world,
I write of love I do not understand,
And haven't come to know.
For here, love is one way.
Reflecting off of mirrors-
until one with me.
In the darkness of hearts,
Nothing is revealed.
Indefinite is the love of humanity,
Unless it is my own.

I wanted to break your heart,
The same way you did the others.
But you had beat me to it.

Wait.

Before you say the words,

Just wait.

Perhaps if you don't say them at all
We can sit here in bliss forever.

Love was not kind to her kind,
The ones who always give.
Some of them had won
the game of love,
But she was never allowed to play.
For they know she would win,
She was a giver, after all.
But the game needed people to lose,
They needed them to fall.

Subtle Meadow Bee.

In this life you will not know me,
A subtle meadow bee.
But return to your past,
And your heart will fill with glee.
For then not now,
I don't know how,
You told your love to me,
And I rejoiced!
For in that life,
You and I were We.

Tomorrow seemed so far,
She felt it in her core.
For everyday, her heart and mind
Would always be at war.
"I tried to love, I did!"
She said in a loud cry,
"But mama they ask me to give,
and I can never wonder why."
She got back up, dusted herself off,
And rose with all her might.
"I should be strong,
I'm sorry mama,
But I had lost the fight."

I already knew the ending,
I've read this story before.
It doesn't end well for me,
I was just hoping
you'd prove me wrong.

Sticks and stones may
break my bones,
But words can hurt
And silence kills.

They were reaching to her,
But never for her.
They were always
trying to find another in her.

She was made to exist,
But not admire.

I will not slow down for life,
So Death kindly sped up for me.
And in that moment,
I learned true love,
One as vast as the sea.

The Date by the Library.

Perhaps I didn't love you,
But I could have.
You cut it off before it started,
I didn't get a chance to
love your flaws.
I never got to be annoyed by how
loud you play your music,
I never got to hate how long you took
to get ready.
I never got to sit in silence and get
you through the dark,
Or roar through life with you.
Instead, I only got to love you
through the color of your eyes.
It isn't fair, I know, but love was a
game I was willing to play.

"Always the right girl"

At the wrong time

The Boy on the Shore

He didn't remember who she was,
Or who he himself was,
for that matter.
Yet there she was,
her face felt like home,
As if her eyes knew him well.
This girl standing over him,
So sure of the unsureness.
It made him feel safe,
But as empty as his mind is,
He was certain that this girl
mattered to him.

It's alright, I think
I've already known.
It's not your fault
the pain is real.
The heartbreak
was too fateful
to be false.

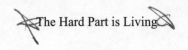

Is it truly love you seek?
Or was it just the feeling
of being wanted?

I love you.
I wanted you to know that.
That word is far too sacred anyway,
So I wanted you to know that
I love you.
In case you haven't heard it today,
I love you.
I love you.
I love you.

At the end of the day,
You are all you have.
So I hope in this journey,
you will learn to love.
I hope you will learn to heal,
I hope you will learn to hurt,
And I hope you will learn to love
everything you are.
The broken porcelain
and the honeystars,
The wonderful and the dark,
The light and the unkown.
I hope you know that all you have
Is more than enough.

Real love began
When you learned
To love the darkness.

The wishing wells will
not do you any good,
The stars you wish on
will not fix you,
and the four-leaf clovers
will not help you.
But the fires you learn
to dance on,
the storms you know
to weather,
and the summers
you spend alone,
will teach you how to love.

So I depart with you this,
May the darkness find you,
May the brightness blind you,
And may the love sting you.
For it is then, when you will learn
To fall in love with being alive
All over again.